# A Busker on Bow Street

Further titles in this series

**Lost Dreams**

**The Farmer's Son**

**The Seasonal Visitor**

# A Busker on Bow Street

Short Stories for Adult Learners No. 1

LinguaBooks Readers

Copyright © 2018 LinguaBooks

The right of the individual authors to be identified as the authors of the stories included in this collection has been asserted in accordance with sections 77 and 78 of the Copyright, Designs and Patents Act 1988.

Published in the United Kingdom by LinguaBooks

ISBN: 978-1-911369-10-3

A CIP catalogue record for this book is available from the British Library.

Series editor: Maurice Claypole
Edited by: Ann Claypole
Proofreader: Marie-Christin Strobel

LinguaBooks
Elsie Whiteley Innovation Centre
Hopwood Lane, Halifax HX1 5ER
www.linguabooks.com

*You don't have anything*
*if you don't have stories*

– Leslie Marmon Silko

# ACKNOWLEDGEMENTS

Some of these stories first appeared in *The Written Word*, a journal for English-speaking residents of Baden-Württemberg, Germany.

The publishers would like to thank the authors of the original stories for offering their work for publication and similarly to express their gratitude to all who were involved in producing both *The Written Word* and the present collection, thereby enabling these stories to reach a wider audience within the context of adult literacy and language learning.

Image credits: cover, page 9, 17, 19, 38 (hearing aid), 50 Dreamstime; 39, 45 Dreamstime & LinguaBooks; 18, 26, 38 (all others), 61 pixabay; 17, 25, 37, 49, 57, 60, 62, 63, 64, 65, 66 LinguaBooks; 51 Le Ramoneur by A. Louis (adapted)

# Contents

# Introduction

This LinguaBooks Reader is the first volume of short stories to be published in this innovative new series.

The stories are presented as originally written by native speakers of English from a variety of countries and backgrounds. Although the punctuation and spelling have largely been harmonised, no attempt has been made to simplify or sanitise the language used. The main objective here is to give learners and other readers an authentic language experience whilst at the same time providing plenty of scope for language acquisition, enhanced awareness and vocabulary expansion. From a point of view of difficulty, the language varies in terms of complexity and register and may be considered equivalent to Level C1 of the Common European Framework of Reference for Languages (CEFR).

The content and scope make each book in this series ideal for classroom use, but the stories can also be read for pleasure, with or without recourse to the supplementary material included. The words and phrases explained after each story provide useful assistance, but lay no claim to completeness, since learners nowadays have ready access to a wide range of external resources. Autonomous learners who favour an active approach will also benefit from the activities and puzzles, which represent a combination of consolidation and discovery exercises. An answer key is provided for the convenience of learners, teachers and independent readers.

# A Busker on Bow Street

## by Bob Oliver

—  ❧ ❧  —

I awoke one spring morning in a cold sweat. Something was gnawing at the back of my mind but just for the moment, I couldn't think what it was. Then it hit me in a stomach-wrenching sort of way, just as I was about to take a bite out of my toast and marmalade. I lost all appetite for my breakfast, but did manage a few gulps of my tea, spilling quite a bit over the tablecloth in the process. The reason for this state of mind was that I suddenly remembered that I was due to appear at Bow Street Magistrates' Court at ten thirty, charged with soliciting for alms by playing a musical instrument at Green Park underground station on such and such a date and I'd clean forgotten about this unwelcome appointment.

A quick look in my wallet revealed the state of my financial affairs. It wasn't a pretty picture. I had just enough for my Tube fare to the famous establishment. Glancing at my watch, I had about enough time to go down the Tube and hopefully busk up the money I would need to pay my fine for busking. Grabbing my guitar, tambourine, mouth organ, kazoo and other bits and pieces, I rushed off to West Kensington Tube station and purchased a ticket with nearly all the money I had left in the world. The last thing I wanted was to be caught without a valid ticket and add further to my woes. Anyway, I jumped onto the District Line and, after changing at Earls Court for the Northern Line, headed towards my destination, Green Park.

I was in luck for a change as there wasn't another busker in sight, but this could also mean the transport cops were about. Still, in for a penny, in for a pound. Choosing my site very carefully, next to the poster warning that busking was not allowed and the maximum fine was twenty-five pounds, I set up my pitch. I must admit I was rather nervous, but I had to make up the money for the fine.

Everything went well. No police turned up, although I heard later they had been on the prowl earlier that morning. The money came in at a steady flow, music to my ears. One tall and distinguished gentleman stopped to listen for quite some time, complimented me on my music and requested 'Where do you go to my lovely' (not me – the song). We had a little chat and he threw fifty pence in my guitar case and carried on his way. By now I'd enough money for my fine, so I gathered my things together and headed reluctantly towards my fate.

I arrived at Bow Street Court with time to spare and sat on a hard, wooden bench with my guitar and things, waiting to be called. This was the calm before the storm and my mind began to wander. I imagined all sorts of things like ending up working on a rock pile or worse. Which was silly really as it was only a bye-law I'd broken. At last my name was called, putting an end to my thoughts.

I stood in the dock alone and awaited the entrance of the magistrate, along with the rest of the court. When he entered, you could have knocked me down with a feather. It was the same tall gentleman who'd paid me a compliment along with fifty pence. I had no choice now but to plead guilty. I waited for the penalty with bated breath as the gentleman, a real gentleman, gave his verdict.

With an evil glint in his eyes and a deep resonant bass voice he said, "Mr. Oliver, shall we say fifty pence?"

I left the court a very happy young man and enough money in my pocket to purchase my next ticket to adventure, busking on the Tube.

— ❧ ❧ —

## Words and phrases

| | |
|---|---|
| *busker* | street musician |
| *gnawing at the back of my mind* | constantly worrying me |
| *stomach-wrenching* | agonising |
| *Bow Street Magistrates' Court* | famous law court in London |
| *soliciting for alms* | begging |
| *wallet* | folding pocketbook for holding money, credit cards, etc. |
| *Tube* | London underground railway |
| *add further to my woes* | give me more problems |
| *in for a penny, in for a pound.* | Now that I have decided to do it, there is no point in stopping. |
| *fine* | financial penalty |
| *the calm before the storm* | peaceful period before things get bad |
| *working on a rock pile* | doing hard labour in prison |
| *bye-law* | local law |
| *the dock* | where the defendant stands in court |
| *magistrate* | judge in a district or county court |
| *plead guilty* | confess to a crime |
| *verdict* | judge's decision |
| *with an evil glint in his eyes* | with a wicked look |

# Food for thought

1. Why does the narrator say, *'Something was gnawing at the back of my mind.'*?
   a. He was looking forward to the day.
   b. He knew it would be a bad day.
   c. He had forgotten something important.

2. *'A quick look in my wallet revealed the state of my financial affairs.'* Which expression best describes his situation?
   a. He is broke.
   b. He is expecting to receive money soon.
   c. He has enough money for his needs.

3. *'I must admit I was rather nervous.'* Why is he feeling nervous?
   a. He has not played in public for a long time.
   b. He is short of time.
   c. He is worried that the police may see him.

4. *'One tall and distinguished gentleman stopped to listen.'* What did the gentleman do?
   a. He asked the busker to stop singing.
   b. He asked the busker to play a certain song.
   c. He gave the busker an unusually large amount of money.

5. *'I left the court a very happy young man.'* Why is he so happy?
   a. He has decided never to break the law again.
   b. He was expecting a much higher fine.
   c. He now knows the standard penalty for busking on the Tube.

# Crossword puzzle

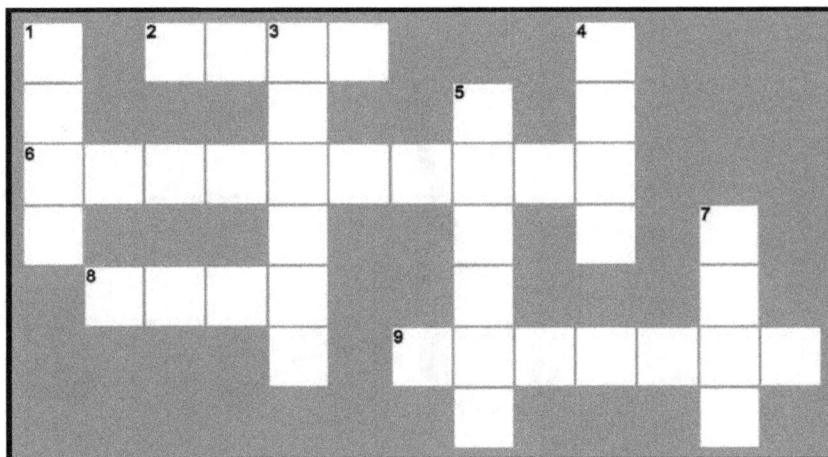

**ACROSS**

**2** London underground railway

**6** judge in a local court

**8** financial penalty

**9** judge's decision

**DOWN**

**1** money given to a beggar

**3** street musician

**4** problems, worries

**5** somewhere to keep your money

**7** where the defendant stands in court

# Picture quiz – musical instruments

**A** Name the instruments (the words are in the story)

1 …………… 2 …………… 3 ……………… 4 ……………

**B** Which of these instruments...

**1** is also called a 'harmonica'?

**2** can you pluck?

**3** can you strike?

**4** makes a buzzing sound?

# The Killer in Me

by Jean Meyer Brandenberg

—— ❦ ❦ ——

I ran in through the back door, throwing the axe down as I entered. The fly-door slammed behind me. I rushed into the bathroom and kicked off my shoes. The lino was cold. I turned on the shower and hoped that the embers in the old stove had kept the water tank warm. I took off my green blouse; blood was spattered all over the front, and it had gone onto my skirt. I felt the blood on my face, it was still warm. I stepped over the edge of the old, white-enamelled iron bath and stood under the shower. The water was reasonably hot. I started to wash the blood out of my hair and off my face. I had to get rid of the evidence. I hadn't killed before. There had to be a first time.

I didn't want anyone to find me like this. I leaned out of the bath, picked up my blouse and skirt and started to feverishly wash out the blood before it stained. Coming to the country like this was certainly not a good idea. Nor was renting this old place. It was cheap, that's true, but it was also a school for killing – a murder scene.

Blood was on my hands. How could I get away from here? My car radiator had boiled dry. I was virtually a prisoner in my own backyard. But I had to get away. I heard noises, the sound of the front door opening and footsteps. "Joan, are you there?" I heard a man's voice call out. I remembered I had invited my friend Dan to come down and visit from the city. I had promised him dinner. I heard him come in. "What on earth is this?" he exclaimed. He walked down the passage, the fly-door opened and shut twice as he went out and came in again. I knew he had seen the blood spots on the lino and the body out in the yard. The game is up, I thought. Better that I confessed to him than to anyone else. I wrapped a towel around me and opened the door. I hoped that there was no more blood on me. Dan stared at me with a grim look on his face. "Don't you know how to kill a chook properly?" he asked, breaking into a smile.

— ❧ ❧ —

## Words and phrases

| | |
|---|---|
| *axe* | a tool with a heavy blade, used for chopping |
| *fly-door* | a screen in a doorway for keeping insects out |
| *slammed* | closed with a bang |
| *lino* | short form of *linoleum*, a hard, washable floor covering |
| *embers* | coal or wood glowing with heat |
| *stove* | apparatus for heating or cooking |
| *white-enamelled* | finished with a hard, white surface |
| *evidence* | sign of a crime, proof |
| *feverishly* | quickly, in a state of panic |
| *stained* | caused permanent marks |
| *car radiator* | part of the cooling system of a car |
| *the game is up* | it's all over |
| *confess* | admit guilt, acknowledge |
| *grim* | stern, serious, severe |
| *chook* | (slang) hen, chicken |

# Food for thought

1.  *'I ... hoped that the embers in the old stove had kept the water tank warm.'* Why does the narrator say this?
    a. It was a cold day and she had just come in from outside.
    b. She needed hot water to get really clean.
    c. It was an old stove that did not always work.

2.  *'I didn't want anyone to find me like this.'* This means she didn't want anyone to see her...
    a. covered in blood.
    b. without any clothes.
    c. living in an old house.

3.  Why is she concerned that her car radiator has boiled dry?
    a. Because she hasn't enough water.
    b. It means she can't escape from where she is.
    c. It isn't really her car and she has to give it back.

4.  Why does she feel that she has to confess?
    a. She knows he has seen blood stains.
    b. Because he has a stern look on his face.
    c. He is a friend, and she had made him a promise.

5.  Which word best describes Dan's reaction when he realises what she has done?
    a. shocked
    b. amused
    c. worried

# Crossword puzzle

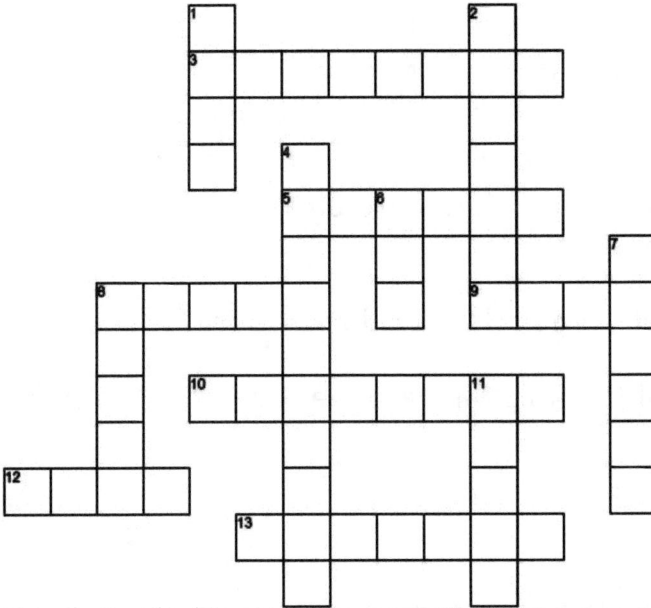

## ACROSS

**3** part of a cooling (or heating) system
**5** hard surface finish, e.g. for metal
**8** used for cooking or heating
**9** shut with a loud noise
**10** legal word for a sign or indication
**12** floor covering
**13** something to keep insects out of a house

**DOWN**: Clues on next page

**DOWN**

**1** harsh, stern, severe
**2** admit responsibility
**4** frantically, in a wild hurry
**6** you can chop wood with this
**7** what glows when the fire is nearly out
**8** mark
**11** a domestic or farmyard bird

## Picture quiz – in and around the house

**A** Which of the following are mentioned in the story?

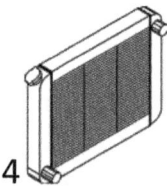

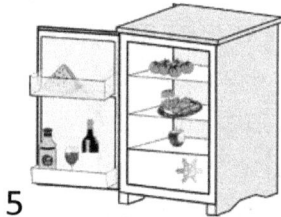

1          2          3

4          5          6

**B** Can you name them? Write the words below.

1 ……………………     2 ……………………     3 ……………………

4 ……………………     5 ……………………     6 ……………………

# Tea for Two

by Anthony Curtis

— ❧ ❧ —

I hesitated before ringing the doorbell and flinched when I heard the trembling voice.

"Who is it?"

"My name is Matthews, Mrs Brent. I moved in yesterday. I have the flat opposite you."

"What do you want?"

"I'm afraid I've run out of sugar."

"Oh dear, it's rather difficult. Never mind. Just a moment, please."

I waited. After a while, a bolt was drawn and a key turned. The door opened. She stood framed in the doorway, epitomising all the sweet old ladies that have ever lived. And I wanted to run.

"You'd better come in, Mr... er..."

"Matthews."

"Oh, yes. I'm afraid I've dropped the sugar. I'm blind, you see."

How glad I was she could not see my face.

"I'm terribly sorry," I said as I entered the room. "May I put the light on?"

"Oh, how silly of me; I forget, you know. The switch is on the left, close to the door."

I switched the light on. I glanced at the living room as we passed through it to the kitchen. I had expected aspidistras and chiffon lace, but was confronted with polished chrome, sheer white and, apart from a pair of pale yellow curtains, a distinct lack of colour.

"May I offer you some tea?" she asked when I had swept up the sugar from the tiled floor. "I do hope you won't feel that I'm being forward, but I seldom have visitors."

I wanted to say no, but couldn't. Months before, when she had been able to see, I had watched her from my window across the street as she tended her plants on the balcony.

In the following months, we often took tea together. We spoke of many things, but she never mentioned the cause of her blindness, and I dared not.

I was struck by her stoicism, by her laughter, which defied her dark loneliness, and when I visited her, she always greeted me with "How nice to see you." To see me!

I told her I was a struggling writer, and she playfully suggested I was using her as a character study. I laughed with her, of course, but inwardly, my soul cried in anguish. I realise now that man is primarily self-centred, that in the final analysis, he thinks only of himself.

Then one bright evening in the summer, in chrome-reflected and white-absorbed sunlight, we met for the last time. I distinctly remember the stain on the tablecloth as I upset my tea.

"You've never learned to live with it, have you?" she said.

"With what?" I spluttered.

She felt for my arm and laid her hand on it.

"Please don't make it harder, young man. Remember the first time you came to see me? You addressed me as Mrs Brent. That was a mistake, my dear. Not long after my accident, my husband passed away and I reverted to my maiden name. I instructed the caretaker to change the name-plate downstairs. How you knew my married name has puzzled me ever since. And you never inquired as to the cause of my blindness. I thought at first that you did not want to be inquisitive, but now I know."

Her fingers grasped my arm in a vice-like grip.

"Why?" she asked. "Why did you come? Has your conscience been pricking you all this time?"

I sat there staring at her unseeing eyes, wishing that I had a stone to crawl under.

"Shall I tell you how often in the last months I have thought of revenge?" People say that it is sweet, but the thought is actually sour. One thing I've learned, however, is that you are suffering more than I am. I've learned to live with my blindness. Can you live with your guilt? Perhaps it will ease your conscience when I tell you that there is a good chance that I will regain my eyesight. The operation is expensive, but I can afford it."

She must have felt the renewed tension in my arm, for she said, "No, I require no further help from you. All those anonymous payments into my account. I wonder how you obtained the number."

Much to my relief she let go of my arm.

The sun had gone and the room was in semi-darkness. I went to the door and switched on the light. I sat down again and she said, "You were drunk that night, weren't you? I'd often read of hit-and-run drivers in the newspapers, but never dreamed of being one of their victims."

Tears streamed down my cheeks. "Please don't," I sobbed.

She laid her hand once more on my arm and began to stroke it.

"Hush," she said softly. "It's over now, no more sleepless nights."

She stood up, her expression hardening as she said, "You'd better go now; it's been a trying experience for us both."

"Will I ever see you again?" I croaked. For God help me, I loved her.

She shrugged. "It's strange, but I can't say yes and I can't say no. It's really up to you, I suppose."

As I went out of the door, I thought I heard her say, "You needn't turn off the light."

—— ❧ ❦ ——

# Words and phrases

| | |
|---|---|
| *hesitate* | pause, be reluctant to act |
| *flinch* | draw back, e.g. from danger |
| *trembling* | shaking, for example with fear |
| *bolt* | locking bar on a door |
| *framed in the doorway* | surrounded by the door frame |
| *epitomising* | serving as a typical example |
| *aspidistra* | large evergreen house plant |
| *chiffon lace* | netlike ornamental fabric |
| *tiled* | covered with hard ceramic squares. |
| *stoicism* | bravery, acting without emotion |
| *my soul cried in anguish* | I was in acute distress |
| *splutter* | speak rapidly when confused or embarrassed |
| *maiden name* | a woman's surname before marriage |
| *inquisitive* | curious, wanting to know |
| *a vice-like grip* | a very tight hold |
| *hit-and-run driver* | a person who causes a traffic accident and then flees from the scene |
| *trying* | difficult |

# Food for thought

1. Why does Matthews say, *'I flinched when I heard the trembling voice.'*?
   - a. He is very nervous and not fully prepared for what might happen next.
   - b. The old woman was rather frightening.
   - c. He did not expect anyone to answer the door.

2. *'Epitomising all the sweet old ladies that have ever lived.'* Why is this important to him?
   - a. It makes it easier for him to talk to her.
   - b. She reminds him of other old ladies from his past.
   - c. It makes him feel worse about what he has done.

3. Why did he expect to see aspidistras and chiffon lace?
   - a. He knows she likes plants and old-style decor.
   - b. Old ladies traditionally have such things.
   - c. He didn't know she was blind.

4. *'Wishing I had a stone to crawl under'* Which word best describes his state of mind at this point?
   - a. ashamed
   - b. terrified
   - c. angry

5. *'It's over now, no more sleepless nights.'* This means that...
   - a. she thinks he can relax because his secret is out.
   - b. everything is all right because she has forgiven him.
   - c. he can sleep more easily because he will never see her again.

# Word search

Find the words in the grid. Words can go horizontally, vertically or diagonally in any direction.

| A | I | N | Q | U | I | S | I | T | I | V | E |
|---|---|---|---|---|---|---|---|---|---|---|---|
| R | G | P | G | Z | K | E | C | A | L | R | H |
| T | L | S | J | C | H | I | F | F | O | N | E |
| S | R | U | T | L | R | K | T | H | T | M | S |
| I | E | L | O | O | K | P | S | Z | R | B | I |
| D | T | L | F | S | I | I | T | R | X | D | T |
| I | T | V | H | L | U | C | G | X | E | T | A |
| P | U | N | L | G | I | L | I | L | F | C | T |
| S | L | Q | N | N | F | N | I | S | R | J | E |
| A | P | A | K | J | R | T | C | A | M | Z | G |
| K | S | R | C | L | G | M | W | H | H | Q | Z |
| T | N | N | B | Z | Q | L | Q | T | P | B | Q |

| anguish | flinch | soul |
|---|---|---|
| aspidistra | hesitate | splutter |
| chiffon | inquisitive | stoicism |
| crawl | lace | tiled |

## Picture quiz – disabilities and special needs

**A** Here are some things used by people with disabilities and special needs. Can you name them?

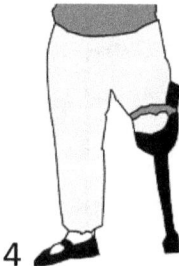

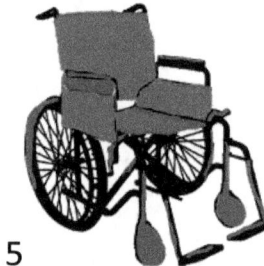

1 ..........................  2 ..........................  3 ..........................

4 ..........................  5 ..........................  6 ..........................

**B** Which of the above might you use if you are

**1** an amputee (  ) **2** a double amputee (  ) **3** blind or paritally sighted (  ) **4** hearing impaired (  ) **5** unable to walk (  ) **6** suffering from a broken ankle (  )

(Put the numbers of the pictures in the brackets)

# The Table

by William David Halbert

— ৯ ৯ —

It's just a table, just an ordinary table. At least in appearance.

It's a simple table, most of a metre high, small grey and white checks on its Formica top, edged with a silver aluminium strip. A simple pedestal table that can be found in coffee shops throughout the country. This particular coffee shop is long closed and the table now stands in a revered corner of my small, dimly lit apartment in this unfashionable part of town; a light in the darkness of this heart's long night.

It was across this very table that I first saw her. To be sure, she was beautiful. And like the legendary Helen whose face launched a thousand ships, her face possessed a mystic quality setting her apart from all others. When she walked into a room, all eyes turned, both men's and women's. Her most amazing feature was her hair. It was satiny and soft as down in texture, a cascade of dark brown, almost black, silk falling to her lower back. Her hair was only one of many distinctive characteristics and perfectly complemented her long, lithe and soft features. Yet her presence, the sheer strength of being – of the radiant soul within – was the driving attraction of this wonder.

As was my usual habit, I sat down at my usual table in my usual cafe for my usual Earl Grey. Yet as soon as I sat down, I was captivated by her as though the rest of the world simply fell away. She was sitting there with a book in hand and a glass of Talisker on the table, her presence warming the rest of the room. The novel she was fixed on, as surely as I was fixed on her, was Spanish. I would learn later on of her passion for all things Spanish – dress, music, food and in particular, these Spanish gothic novels. There was one exception to this fascination – her love of Scottish single malts, Talisker in particular. So it was when I first saw her: her beauty, her Spanish novel, her Talisker. But she had not taken notice of me, nor had she reason to. Instead, after a while, she paid her bill and left.

It was then that I first noticed how the table took on an appearance different from the others. It seemed translucent – as if of its own power, or possibly from some faint remnant of her presence, it began to glow, its surface shining like pearl in the midst of a grey plastic ocean. How could I but move to it as it called out to me? Putting my hand on the table, I felt the wondrous though strange warmth invading my senses. It was as though the table physically held me to it. I was unable to be free, yet content to be captive. Sitting there, I was startled as she returned, looking for her key. As if by some kind of magic, I could feel her key in my hand, its smooth and jagged edges pressing into my skin as if put there by some unseen force. Truly, the key had not been there before as I had admired the table's smoothness and emptiness, a perfect metaphor of my own life. Yet in my hand was the key. I gave it to her as she sat down at what was now our table. In gratitude, she called the waiter and ordered two more Taliskers. I remember nothing of what was said. I see only her beautiful hair shining, eyes flashing, skin glowing. If only I could reach out and become part of this scene once more... Whenever we went out it was always to that cafe, and always to that table, our table. Oh, what that table saw and heard! It witnessed our happiness, our sorrows and even my nervous hand's fumbling when I proffered the ring for her eternal hand. So many times we returned, even after we had in delight exchanged our vows for a lifetime together.

I shall not tell the details of her tragic, sudden and untimely death as in the telling the pain of her passing comes back to life. Only know that the wind swept her away from me, leaving me lost and alone. It was not until years later, when I heard of the cafe's demise that I set eyes again on our table. The door was ajar on the condemned building, slated for the wrecking ball, when I entered. Years of misuse followed by years of disuse had claimed their toll on the cafe. Scattered rocks lay on the floor next to shards of glass their throwers had broken. Dust was everywhere and a certain damp mustiness emanating from the rotting beams lingered in the air, stifling my breath, suffocating all sound. The few chairs and tables that remained were broken and scattered around. Only the bar at the end of the room was intact, though thickly covered with a layer of grime.

Then I spied a very singular, dim glow emanating from a point just out of sight behind the bar. As I approached, the familiar, warm and eerie glow grew greater with every step. Once again the table called out to me. When it had done so before it had, for a time, saved my life. Only now I was able to return the favour. I left the café, knowing I would never set foot in it again.

Through my tears I could see my true love's face as if again we met for the very first time.

—— ❧ ❧ ——

# Words and phrases

| | |
|---|---|
| *Formica* | type of hard plastic covering |
| *pedestal table* | table with one central leg |
| *revered* | regarded with great respect |
| *satiny* | smooth, glossy, like satin/silk |
| *cascade* | falling in stages, like a waterfall |
| *lithe* | elegant, flexible, supple |
| *radiant* | shining, bright, giving off light |
| *Earl Grey* | tea flavoured with oil of bergamot |
| *captivated* | fascinated, enchanted |
| *single malt* | an unblended Scotch whisky |
| *translucent* | allowing light to pass through |
| *demise* | death, closing down, passing |
| *ajar* | partly open |
| *condemned* | declared unfit for use |
| *invading my senses* | taking over my feelings |
| *jagged* | rough, uneven, zigzag |
| *in gratitude* | as a way of saying thank you |
| *claimed their toll* | had a damaging effect |
| *shards* | fragments |
| *mustiness* | stale or mouldy smell |
| *lingered in the air* | remained, stayed, hung around |
| *grime* | dirt clinging to a surface |
| *eerie* | strange, mysterious, weird |

# Food for thought

1. *'In a revered corner of my ... apartment'* Why does the writer use the word 'revered'?
    a. Because part of his apartment contains a valuable antique.
    b. Because he is a deeply religious person.
    c. To show that something is special to him.

2. Why does he compare her to *'the legendary Helen'*?
    a. Because her hair is like Helen's.
    b. Because she likes to read classical literature.
    c. Because he finds her extremely beautiful.

3. What happened after she left the cafe?
    a. He found a key on the floor.
    b. The table seemed to change.
    c. He had a dream.

4. *'When I proffered the ring for her eternal hand.'* What kind of ring is meant here?
    a. a wedding ring
    b. an engagement ring
    c. a magic ring

5. *'Only now, I was able to return the favour.'* What does this tell us?
    a. He decided to rescue the table from destruction.
    b. He knew he would never see the table again.
    c. It was not really the same table.

# Crossword

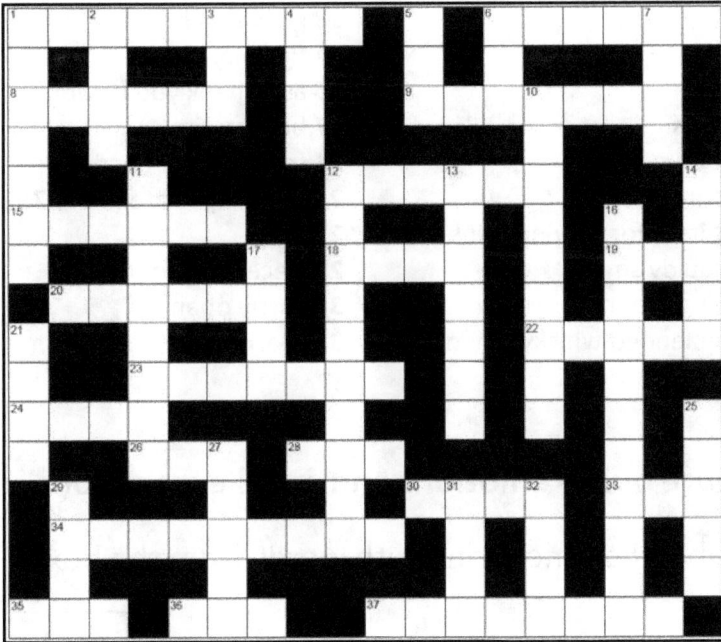

## ACROSS

**1** declared unfit
**6** Helen of Troy was famous for her ...
**8** smooth, glossy
**9** hard plastic covering
**12** fragments
**15** death
**18** require
**19** mesh, item used for catching fish
**20** rough, uneven

**22** weird
**23** regarded with respect
**24** place to eat and drink
**26** canine animal
**28** feline animal
**30** be unsuccessful
**33** plaything
**34** enchant
**35** attempt
**36** thing for opening a lock
**37** type of tea (2 words)

## DOWN: Clues on next page

49

## DOWN

**1** fall in stages
**2** message, record
**3** month
**4** always
**5** not on
**6** serving area
**7** flat item for serving drinks, etc.
**10** mouldy smell
**11** hung around
**12** unblended whisky (2 words)

**13** giving off light
**14** flexible, supple
**16** as a thank you (2 words)
**17** border, rim
**21** front part of head
**25** film, deposit, e.g. of 27
**27** dirt
**29** trace of a wound
**31** partly open
**32** yearn

## Picture quiz – emotions and facial expressions

**A** Label the emoticons with words from the box.

**1** ......... **2** ......... **3** ... ..... **4** ........... **5** ........

| sad   in love |
| aghast  furious |
| happy |

**B** In which of the images below is someone...?

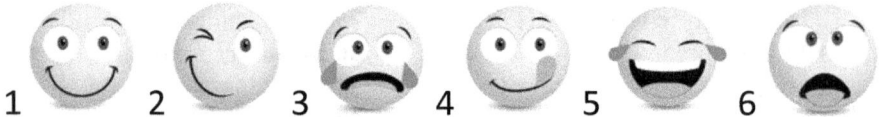

**1** ........ **2** ........ **3** ........ **4** ........ **5** ........ **6** ........

**1** sobbing (   ) **2** licking their lips (   ) **3** winking (   )
**4** shedding tears of joy (   )  **5** sticking their tongue out in
disgust (   ) **6** smiling from ear to ear (   )

# Blacky

by Anthony Curtis

— ❧ ❧ —

Every village, every town, every city he visited lacked what he was looking for, and his frustration was immense. Until one day he was lucky. How and why (if you're not inclined to cheat) is explained at the end of this story.

He was born in the year 2200 and died eighteen years later. By 2214 he knew exactly what he was going to be. He had visited an antique shop and found an ancient picture book. An old man, (who was himself almost an antique), let him have it for next to nothing, for no-one bought such things any more.

The crucial moment came in 2216, when, pressed to choose a career, he had an argument with his parents.

"That is what I want to be," he said, showing them one of the pictures in the book.

"What?" asked father, and mother swooned on the water bed.

Revived, mother said, "But you can't. They're not needed any more."

"Don't you understand, son?" said father. "They're extinct."

"I don't care. That's what I want to be. Even if it means starvation or worse."

With tears and threats and a final handout, he set off on his quest.

By 2217, he was ready to give up; but then he found what he was looking for; in another antique shop. This time the article was expensive; the dealer said it was the only one left in the world. The accessories he could have for nothing. The searcher willingly gave almost all of his money to the dealer, who shook his head and stared in wonder at the apparition that now stood before him.

This apparition marched jauntily through the streets while jeering inhabitants followed him to the outskirts of the town.

"You don't exist any more," said an old man.

"You're extinct," said another.

"You've got bats in the belfry," said a young woman.

He hastened his steps and soon left the people behind him.

He wandered and wandered, for there was still something that he needed; and in April 2218, with a great whoop of joy, he found it.

A tall, thin tower, attached to an ancient ruin. It was the only structure he had ever seen that did not have hundreds of panels to soak up the sun's energy. The tower was about thirty feet high and had steel rungs jutting out of it. He fastened his paraphernalia and began to climb.

When he reached the top, he began to descend the tower from the inside.

On reaching the bottom, he fell asleep from exhaustion, never to wake again.

While he was asleep, an explosion occurred, and the tower he had climbed fell slowly but surely to the ground, like the Tower of Pisa had done a hundred years earlier.

Later, when the dust had settled, a group of men with steel helmets gathered round the thing that had been flung out by the force of the explosion.

"I thought they didn't exist any more," said one of the men.

"So did I," said another, and stared at the body of a young man dressed as a chimney sweep.

And the youngster's face was as black as a starless night.

Later, a plaque was unveiled on the site of the tragedy...

Here lie the remains
of the last chimney sweep in the world.
He had obviously been born two hundred
years too late; for the world has been
powered by solar energy for the last
hundred and fifty years.

Let the death of this young man be a
lesson to us all. We must walk boldly into
the Future, and not retreat into the Past,
for that is the way to destruction

This plaque was laid by His Excellency
The World President

Anno Domini 2218.

— ෩ ෪ —

# Words and phrases

| | |
|---|---|
| *lacked* | did not have |
| *crucial* | extremely important, critical |
| *pressed* | put under pressure, urged |
| *swooned* | fainted |
| *extinct* | no longer existing |
| *quest* | mission, expedition, search |
| *accessories* | additional articles or parts, e.g. of an outfit |
| *apparition* | figure, person of unusual appearance |
| *jauntily* | happily and with confidence |
| *jeering* | mocking, shouting insults |
| *you've got bats in the belfry* | you're crazy |
| *whoop* | loud, excited shout of joy |
| *rungs* | bars used as steps of a ladder |
| *jutting out* | sticking out, protruding |
| *paraphernalia* | equipment, apparatus |
| *flung out* | thrown out |
| *chimney sweep* | a person who cleans chimneys for a living |
| *plaque* | commemorative sign on a wall |
| *unveiled* | revealed, shown for the first time |

# Food for thought

1. How did his parents react when he told them of his plans?
   a. They didn't understand what he wanted to do.
   b. They were very happy for him.
   c. They tried to talk him out of it.

2. What happened in 2217?
   a. He started out on his search.
   b. He bought something.
   c. He abandoned his quest.

3. What was special about the tower?
   a. It was a very old and rare type of structure.
   b. It was made partly of steel.
   c. It had hundreds of solar panels.

4. What happened to the tower?
   a. It was destroyed by a team of workmen.
   b. It collapsed under his weight.
   c. I was struck by a flying object.

5. Which sentence best sums up the message of the plaque?
   a. The future is always better than the past.
   b. Look forward, do not look back.
   c. The world is now united under a single government.

# Word search

Find the words in the grid. Words can go horizontally, vertically or diagonally in any direction.

When you are done, the unused letters in the grid will spell out a hidden message, reading from left to right, top to bottom. There will be a few letters left over.

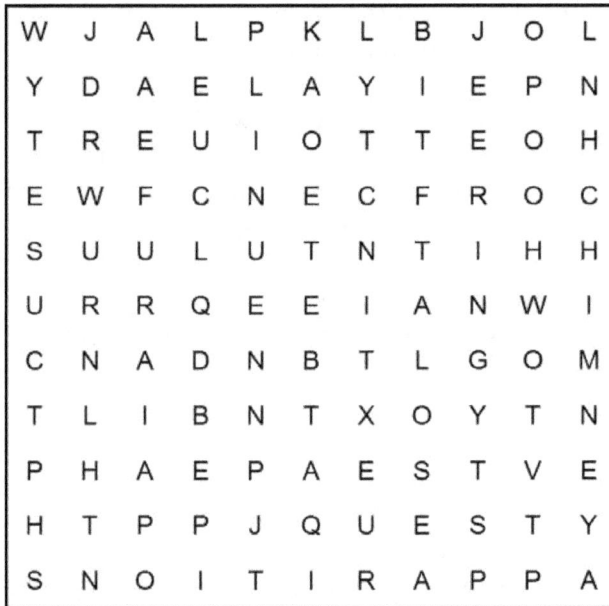

| W | J | A | L | P | K | L | B | J | O | L |
|---|---|---|---|---|---|---|---|---|---|---|
| Y | D | A | E | L | A | Y | I | E | P | N |
| T | R | E | U | I | O | T | T | E | O | H |
| E | W | F | C | N | E | C | F | R | O | C |
| S | U | U | L | U | T | N | T | I | H | H |
| U | R | R | Q | E | E | I | A | N | W | I |
| C | N | A | D | N | B | T | L | G | O | M |
| T | L | I | B | N | T | X | O | Y | T | N |
| P | H | A | E | P | A | E | S | T | V | E |
| H | T | P | P | J | Q | U | E | S | T | Y |
| S | N | O | I | T | I | R | A | P | P | A |

apparition

bats

belfry

chimney

crucial

extinct

jauntily

jeering

plaque

quest

sweep

whoop

Hidden message: ..............................................................

60

# Picture quiz – jobs and occupations

**A** Unscramble the words below and match them to the pictures.

PRETRANCE - TIDNEST - DINWOW RENACLE - FECH
REBKA - COTROD - REBLUMP - GORTHOHPAPER

Write the words below.

1 …………….. 2 …………….. 3 …………….. 4 ……………..
5 …………….. 6 …………….. 7 …………….. 8 ……………..

**B** Match the equipment with the occupations. Answer by putting the numbers in the brackets

**1** tripod ( ) **2** stethoscope ( ) **3** oven ( ) **4** plunger ( )
**5** squeegee ( ) **6** scaler ( ) **7** frying pan ( ) **8** jigsaw ( )

# Answer key

## A Busker on Bow Street

*Food for thought*
**1** c   **2** a   **3** c   **4** b   **5** b

*Crossword puzzle*

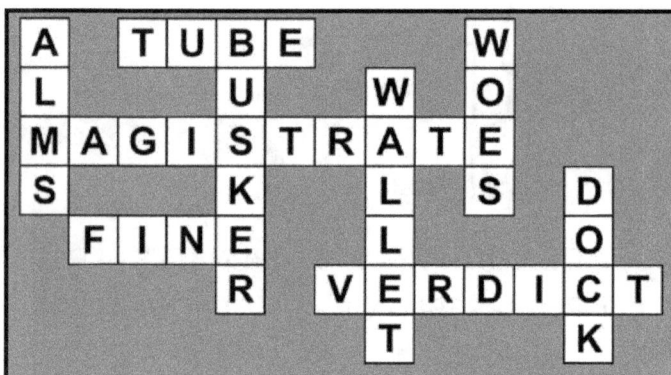

|   |   |   |   |   |   |   |   |   |   |
|---|---|---|---|---|---|---|---|---|---|
| A |   | T | U | B | E |   |   | W |   |
| L |   |   | U |   |   | W |   | O |   |
| M | A | G | I | S | T | R | A | T | E |
| S |   |   | K |   |   | L |   | S | D |
|   | F | I | N | E |   | L |   |   | O |
|   |   |   | R |   | V | E | R | D | I | C | T |
|   |   |   |   |   | T |   |   | K |   |

*Picture quiz*

**A**
**1** tambourine   **2** guitar   **3** kazoo   **4** mouth organ

**B**
**1** mouth organ   **2** guitar   **3** tambourine   **4** kazoo

# The Killer in Me

*Food for thought*
**1** b   **2** a   **3** b   **4** a   **5** b

*Crossword puzzle*

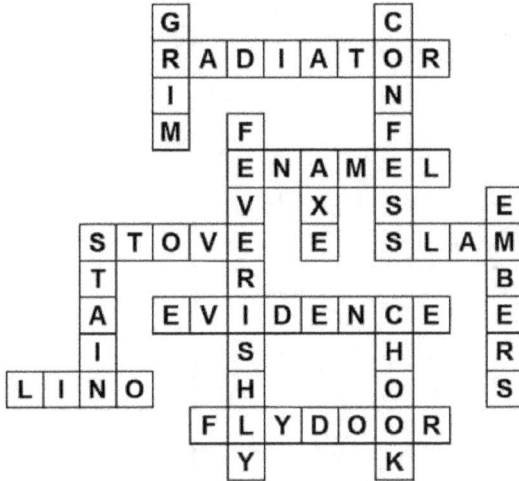

```
    G          C
    R A D I A T O R
    I          N
    M   F      F
        E N A M E L
        V   X   S     E
S T O V E   E   S L A M
T       R           B
A   E V I D E N C E   E
  I     S       H     R
L I N O H       O     S
        F L Y D O O R
        Y       K
```

*Picture quiz*

**A**

**1, 3** and **4** are mentioned in the story.

**B**

**1** bath and shower   **2** pullover/sweater   **3** hen/chicken/chook
**4** car radiator   **5** refrigerator/fridge   **6** gun/revolver

# Tea for Two

*Food for thought*

**1** a   **2** c   **3** b   **4** a   **5** a

*Word search*

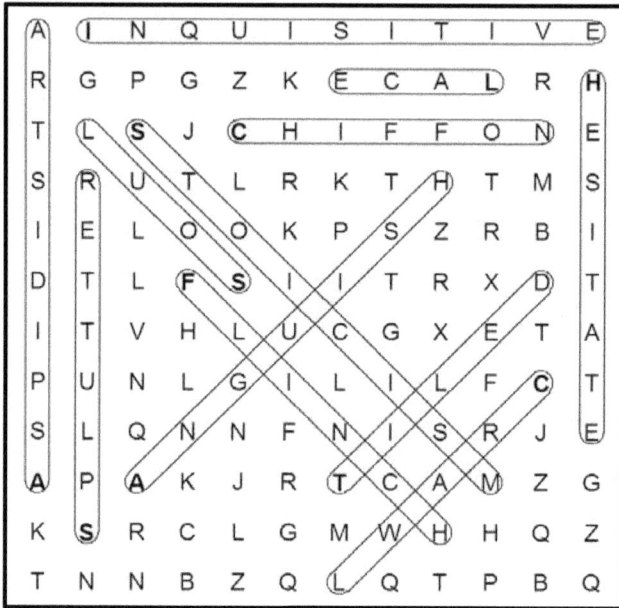

*Picture quiz*

**A**

**1** white stick/cane   **2** crutch   **3** hearing aid   **4** wooden leg / peg
leg   **5** wheelchair   **6** running blades

**B**

**1** (4)   **2** (6)   **3** (1)   **4** (3)   **5** (5)   **6** (2)

# The Table

*Food for thought*
**1** c  **2** c  **3** b  **4** b  **5** a

*Crossword puzzle*

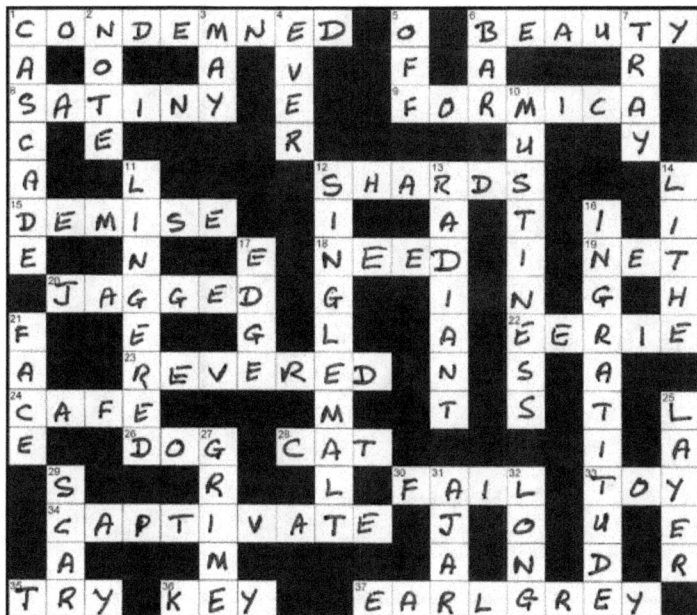

| C | O | N | D | E | M | N | E | D |   | O |   | B | E | A | U | T | Y |
|---|---|---|---|---|---|---|---|---|---|---|---|---|---|---|---|---|---|
| A |   | O |   |   | A |   | V |   | F |   | A |   |   |   |   | R |   |
| S | A | T | I | N | Y |   | E |   | F | O | R | M | I | C | A |   |   |
| C |   | E |   |   | R |   |   |   |   |   | M |   |   |   | Y |   |   |
| A |   | L |   |   |   | S | H | A | R | D | S |   |   |   |   | L |   |
| D | E | M | I | S | E |   | I |   | A |   | T |   | I |   |   | I |   |
| E |   | N |   | E |   | N | E | E | D |   | I |   | N | E | T |   |   |
|   | J | A | G | G | E | D |   | G |   | I |   | N | G |   | H |   |   |
| F |   | E |   | G |   | L |   | A |   | E | E | R | I | E |   |   |   |
| A |   | R | E | V | E | R | E | D |   | N |   | S |   | A |   |   |   |
| C | A | F | E |   |   | M |   |   |   | T |   | S |   | T |   | L |   |
| E |   | D | O | G |   | C | A | T |   |   | I |   |   |   | A |   |   |
|   | S |   | R |   | L |   | F | A | I | L |   | T | O | Y |   |   |   |
| C | A | P | T | I | V | A | T | E |   | J |   | O |   | U |   | E |   |
| A |   | M |   |   |   |   |   | A |   | O |   | N |   | D |   | R |   |
| T | R | Y |   | K | E | Y |   | E | A | R | L | G | R | E | Y |   |   |

*Picture quiz*

**A**

**1** in love  **2** sad  **3** aghast  **4** happy  **5** furious

**B**

**1** (3)  **2** (4)  **3** (2)  **4** (5)  **5** (6)  **6** (1)

# Blacky

*Food for thought*

**1** c  **2** b  **3** a  **4** a  **5** b

*Word search*

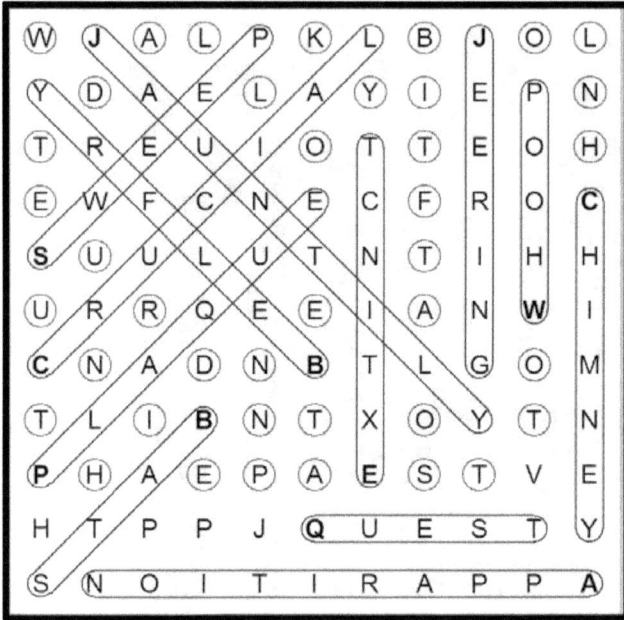

Hidden message: WALK BOLDLY INTO THE FUTURE
 AND NOT INTO THE PAST

*Picture quiz*

**A**

**1** DOCTOR  **2** CHEF  **3** CARPENTER  **4** BAKER  **5** PLUMBER
**6** WINDOW CLEANER  **7** PHOTOGRAPHER  **8** DENTIST

**B**

**1** (7)  **2** (1)  **3** (4)  **4** (5)  **5** (6)  **6** (8)  **7** (2)  **8** (3)

# Further titles from LinguaBooks

## IN A STRANGE LAND
Short Stories for Creative Learning
*Andrzej Cirocki and Alicia Peña Calvo*       ISBN 978-3734789465

IN A STRANGE LAND is a collection of four original short stories which provide teachers with motivating and engaging classroom material at the CEFR B2 to C1 level and young adult learners with thought-provoking narratives and characters to whom they can relate.

This gripping teenage fiction encourages readers to use their imagination and interact with the texts in a variety of educational and experimental ways.

The stories are supported by creative tasks which enable students to integrate their various language skills, exploit computer technology, practise learning strategies and exercise autonomy.

Audio recordings of the stories are available on two separate CDs which are suitable for classroom use and can also be listened to for pleasure.


## Academic Presenting and Presentations
A preparation course for university students
*Peter Levrai and Averil Bolster*       ISBN 978-3734783678

This practical training course is designed to help students cultivate academic presentation skills and deal with the variety of presentation tasks they may need to master during their studies.

The material is suitable for a global audience and can be used in a wide range of academic contexts since the content not only helps learners develop their presentation skills in English but also considers wider topics relevant to English for Academic Purposes, such as principles of research and the risk of plagiarism.

The accompanying online video presentations enable learners to immerse themselves still further in the material presented and witness first-hand the impact of the techniques illustrated.

A separate Teacher's Book is also available:       ISBN: 978-3741242090

## Developing Learner Autonomy Through Tasks
Theory, Research, Practice
*Andrzej Cirocki*                                    ISBN 978-1-911369-01-1

At the heart of this study is the fostering of learner autonomy in the language classroom, in particular how learner autonomy can be developed through pedagogical tasks. The work focuses on four different approaches: learner-related, classroom-related, resource-related and technology-related.

**Developing Learner Autonomy through Tasks** combines classroom theory, research and practice, all of which are immersed in the philosophy of social constructivism, whereby knowledge and learning are seen as both the context for and the result of human interaction.

*"This is the book everyone in the field has been waiting for. It is the product of excellent classroom research... highly engaging, relevant, readable, and above all, practical in its handling of the issues."*
- Prof. John McRae, University of Nottingham, UK


## Controversies in ELT
What you always wanted to know about teaching English
but were afraid to ask
*Maurice Claypole*                                    ISBN 978-1-911369-00-4

This thought-provoking and informative collection of essays covers a broad spectrum of topics relating to English language teaching, including chapters on The Death Of the Communicative Approach, Teaching the Language of Sex and Teaching English in Second Life.

Also released for the first time in book form are chapters on the author's unique insight into the correlation between language, set theory and fractal mathematics - and the consequences for English teachers.

*"This book provides a refreshing look at old concepts, opens our eyes to new perspectives and encourages teachers to venture along new paths."*
- Elke Schulth, ELTAS, Germany

*"Interesting... instructive and - not least - fun to read. A brilliant book!"*
- Nick Michelioudakis, TESOL Greece

www.ingramcontent.com/pod-product-compliance
Lightning Source LLC
LaVergne TN
LVHW051710080426
835511LV00017B/2827